THE UNDERGROUND RAILROAD

A HISTORY PERSPECTIVES BOOK

Sheila Griffin Llanas

Published in the United States of America by Cherry Lake Publishing
Ann Arbor, Michigan
www.cherrylakepublishing.com

Consultants: Ibram H. Rogers, PhD, Assistant Professor, Africana Studies
Department, University at Albany, SUNY; Marla Conn, ReadAbility, Inc.
Editorial direction: Red Line Editorial
Book design and illustration: Sleeping Bear Press

Photo Credits: Library of Congress, cover (left), cover (middle), cover
(right), 1 (left), 1 (middle), 1 (right), 6, 18; AP Images, 4; North Wind/
North Wind Picture Archives, 12, 14, 17, 22, 24, 30; Renee Sauer/Columbus
Dispatch/AP Images, 13; H. B. Lindsley/Library of Congress, 27

Library of Congress Cataloging-in-Publication Data
Llanas, Sheila Griffin, 1958-
  The Underground Railroad / Sheila Griffin Llanas.
     pages cm. – (Perspectives library)
  ISBN 978-1-62431-423-0 (hardcover) – ISBN 978-1-62431-499-5 (pbk.)
– ISBN 978-1-62431-461-2 (pdf) – ISBN 978-1-62431-537-4 (ebook)
  1. Underground Railroad – Juvenile literature. 2. Fugitive slaves – United
States – History – 19th century – Juvenile literature. 3. Antislavery
movements – United States – History – 19th century – Juvenile literature.
I. Title.
E450.L63 2014
973.7'115–dc23
                         2013006437

Cherry Lake Publishing would like to acknowledge the work of
The Partnership for 21st Century Skills. Please visit www.p21.org
for more information.

Printed in the United States of America
Corporate Graphics Inc.
July 2013
CLFA11

TABLE OF CONTENTS

In this book, you will read about the Underground Railroad from three perspectives. Each perspective is based on real things that happened to real people who experienced or were linked to the Underground Railroad. As you'll see, the same event can look different depending on one's point of view.

1

Josiah Braxton
Runaway Slave

The older slaves told me I am 17. They say my mother's mother came on a ship from Africa. I thought I'd live my whole life on the Kentucky farm where I grew up. My life as a slave was hard. We worked six days a week, from sunup to sundown. We slept in leaky shacks and were given just the bare essentials to live. But my life was not as hard as I knew it was for slaves in the Deep South. There they live in even poorer conditions and faced more beatings than we did on the farm.

My master died one full moon ago, and all of his property was transferred into his widow's hands. She and her son began selling field hands. To them, we were their legal property. We had no rights. I saw a husband sold from his wife. I saw three young men like me taken in chains, headed for a cotton **plantation** in Alabama. I made a promise to myself that I would not be sold off like a horse. I refused to go to the Deep South, farther from freedom and deeper into the places where slavery is the most cruel.

My chance to keep that promise came sooner than I expected. While working in the fields, I heard another slave, Dotty, sing. The birds, rivers, and stars in her songs are the coded language of the Underground Railroad. Dotty helps slaves escape from this farm and from other farms too. That makes her a conductor. When she turns the farm into an Underground Railroad **depot**, she is a station master. She feeds **fugitives** who hide in the forest far behind the farm's cabins.

I vowed that I would go to freedom too, but I knew it would be hard. An older field hand told me I would have to walk hundreds of miles to the Ohio

▲ *Traveling the Underground Railroad was dangerous for runaway slaves.*

River and cross it in order to get into Ohio, a free state. The slave catchers had dogs that might be sniffing my trail, trying to find me. If they caught me, the slave catchers would make my life a nightmare. It couldn't be any worse than going to the Deep South, I thought.

The night I was ready to go, I slept a few hours and awoke when Dotty shook me. She gave me stale bread and told me to sneak through the woods. She instructed me to hide during the day, walk at night, and always keep the North Star in front of me. After four nights, I should look for a white house with a green roof and five front steps. The couple who live there would help me. With those instructions, I slipped into the night. The moment my foot touched the ground, I was on the Underground Railroad.

My passage has been lonely. I am hungry, cold, and afraid. To ease my mind, I go over what I know about the Underground Railroad. Conductors are

HOW THE UNDERGROUND RAILROAD GOT ITS NAME

Several stories exist about how the Underground Railroad got its name. In one story, a slave owner feverishly chased a runaway slave all the way to the Ohio River. The fugitive swam across the river and crawled up on the other side. The slave owner watched in disbelief. He said it was as if he had disappeared on an "underground railroad."

people who guide slaves trying to escape from slavery. Churches and homes along the way are stations. People willing to hide slaves like me who are on the run are station masters.

Late into the fourth night, I find the house and sleep close by. At dawn, I hear a bird call and see a man standing on the porch. Terrified, I creep from my hiding place. It is a big risk. What if he is a slave catcher?

Jesse is his name. He is a farmer and introduces me to his wife, Laura. I am in Maysville, Kentucky, they tell me. The town is very near the Ohio River and just south of Ripley, Ohio. They whisk me into the house. Laura feeds me a bowl of warm soup. After I eat, Jesse takes me to a hidden closet. I sleep all day on a great pile of blankets.

SECOND SOURCE

▶ Find another source that discusses what happened when a fugitive slave reached a stop on the Underground Railroad. How is it similar to the account described here? How is it different?

That evening, Jesse says it is safe for me to come out. He allows me a place at the family table next to his three children. I have never been treated so kindly by white people. I listen to a lively conversation while I eat.

Jesse says there are many routes and **modes** of travel on the Underground Railroad. Frederick

Douglass escaped slavery by pretending to be a sailor in 1838. Laura mentions that last year, in 1849, a slave mailed himself in a wooden box from Virginia to Philadelphia. After a 27-hour train ride, his box was delivered to the Pennsylvania Anti-Slavery Society. Now he is known as Henry "Box" Brown.

After dinner, Jesse began reading aloud from the *Liberator*. He tells me it was one of many **abolitionist** newspapers. I never knew such things existed. Excited by my interest, Jesse reads from the "Declaration of Sentiments," written by William Lloyd Garrison in 1833. It says that, under the U.S. Constitution, all people should be free. All laws protecting slavery should be "null and void," meaning useless.

But, Jesse says, laws holding up slavery have gotten worse. The new Fugitive Slave Act means there is no safe place for me in our country. Slave owners can find their escaped slaves who have gone to northern states—where slavery is illegal—and bring them back to the South. I would need to go to Canada to truly be free. This act states that slave owners can arrest fugitives like me even when we get to free states. This makes me nervous, and I am anxious to continue my journey. But Jesse must prepare my passage and wait for the signal. On the Underground Railroad, he says, safety is more important than speed.

THINK ABOUT IT

▶ What is the main idea of this paragraph? Provide evidence to support your answer.

Late that night, I am brought back to my hiding place. The next day at sunset, Jesse tells me all is ready. I hide under hay bales in the back of a cart. After a short, bumpy road, the horses stop, and I lift my head. I see the river, and on the other side, Ohio, a free state.

A man near shore waits for me in a boat. He has agreed to row me across. I bid farewell to Jesse and focus on the light across the water. The man tells me

▲ *Even if runaway slaves made it to free states, slave owners could bring them back to the South.*

Reverend John Rankin knows I am coming and has lit the lantern for our arrival. He and his wife, Jean, are Ohio's most active abolitionists.

As we reach shore, the man cautions me. Ohio may be a free state, but it is not safe. Slave catchers patrol the riverbanks. Once out of the boat, I climb the 100 steps to reach the small, red house at the top of the hill. When I knock on the door, a thin, gray-haired man welcomes me and lets me inside. Before he closes the door, I glance back over my shoulder. Across the river is slavery.

I am a slave no more. Slave owners may call me a fugitive and slave catchers may try to find me, but in my heart, I am free.

▲ *This modern-day image shows John and Jean Rankin's home, where many slaves stayed while traveling on the Underground Railroad.*

Thomas Fulton

Slave Owner

My tobacco farm in Tennessee lies 300 miles from Ohio, the nearest free state. Fugitive slaves must cross all of Kentucky to reach the Ohio River. It's a long, dangerous journey, and I'm proud to say my house slaves and field hands have no reason to try it. For one thing, I treat them fairly. For another, they don't have the resources needed to run. They own neither warm clothing nor shoes. Few can read or write and none have seen a map. They fear the punishment of escaping. Until this year, 1851, no slave of mine has ever run away.

My cousin has a cotton plantation in Georgia. He owns 120 slaves and still needs more. I have more hands than I can support. On my cousin's request, I was going to sell him two of my field hands. I knew better than to inform my field hands of their sale. They know southern plantation life can be harder than it is on my farm. But those slaves must have learned they were getting moved. The next day, on the day they were to go to Georgia, those two were gone.

Trading slaves is a business matter. Cotton makes up half our nation's total exports, and the southern states that grow cotton need the labor. Field hands harvest cotton crops. Slaves are the best type of labor we have. So you see, slavery is necessary for our nation's economic growth. Southern politicians

ANALYZE THIS

▶ In another chapter, find a place that discusses slavery's purpose and meaning. How are the two viewpoints alike? How are they different?

agree. No civilized society can exist without a **hierarchy**.

Once I realized my two slaves were fugitives, I acted quickly to recover my property. I hired slave catchers. They are professionals who earn their living catching runaways. I posted a notice in town and placed an ad in the local newspaper. I would give a reward of five dollars for each slave brought back to me.

It is my right to reclaim my property, and it has been my right since 1793, when Congress passed the Fugitive Slave Act. George Washington himself signed that early bill into law. Just a year ago, President Millard Fillmore signed the **Compromise** of 1850. Southern politicians agreed to let California become a new free state. Northern politicians agreed to the new Fugitive Slave Act. This act

▲ *Many slaves picked cotton on plantations in the South.*

strengthened laws that allowed for the capture of runaway slaves.

Kentucky Senator Henry Clay said all citizens and law officers must "assist in the recovery of a fugitive slave from labor, who takes refuge in or escapes into one of the free States." If my slaves are making their way north, by the law's aid, they should be caught.

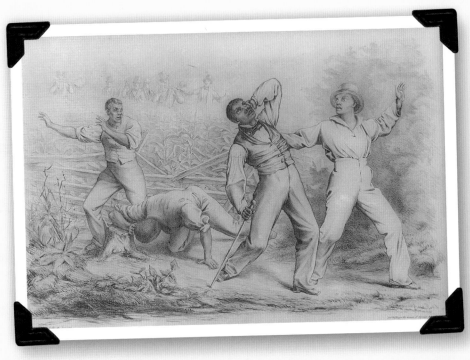

▲ *Slave owners had the right to capture runaway slaves.*

They will come back in chains, captured by lawmen or slave catchers.

Few places in Tennessee or Kentucky will shelter a runaway. Some fugitives never get far. They lurk in the woods near other farms. They depend on friends and family to sneak them food. Many return home after a few days, tired and hungry, after learning they cannot survive as wanted fugitives.

If those fugitives get illegal assistance, it will likely be only along the borders of free states. If by chance they cross the Ohio River, I've heard they may find shelter in churches and farmhouses. But even in the free state of Ohio, they are not safe.

We farmers have all heard stories about a secret system. Fugitives travel at night. They look for lamps in windows or quilts on fences, which signal safe places. Abolitionists guide fugitives to homes and barns, where they hide in secret rooms behind walls. They get hot food, warm blankets, and safe rides to Canada. These sound like made-up stories to me. If it does exist, I'm not too worried about it. This secret system can't free that many slaves this way.

In spite of our nation's need for labor in the South, unpatriotic abolitionists continue to publish anti-slavery newspapers. They oppose slavery on **principles**, not reality. They disrespect the law. The way they insist on harming our agriculture and our way of life is criminal.

THE RANKIN HOUSE

John Rankin once said, "My house has been the door of freedom to many human beings." He and his wife, Jean, gave safe shelter to about 2,000 fugitive slaves. Today, the Rankin House in Ripley, Ohio, is a National Historic Landmark. Visitors can still climb the 100 steps from the river to the house.

The abolitionists have even stooped to printing fiction. Only last week, on June 5, 1851, the *National Era* printed the first chapter of *Uncle Tom's Cabin* by a woman named Harriet Beecher Stowe. Mrs. Stowe's fictional account of slavery will only fuel abolitionists in the north.

With the help of a professional slave catcher and a pack of dogs, I will retrieve my property. They will be punished. And so will anyone who assists them, with fines and jail time.

When they are returned, they will not find life so rosy. No more Sunday afternoons for loafing. No extra food supplies on Saturdays. No permission to leave the farm. Having lost my trust, they will lose those privileges.

THINK ABOUT IT

▶ What is the main idea of this chapter? In what ways do the main idea and details of the chapter surprise you?

3

Emma Jackson

Conductor

In the middle of the night, a knock on the door wakes us from sleep. We rise from bed. Passengers have arrived on the Underground Railroad. My husband opens the door. A man and a woman with a baby stand on our doorstep in the dark, cold night.

Without a sound, we hurry them into the cabin. My husband fastens the door, and I pull the curtains across the windows. We never know who may be watching.

Fear and shock flood the woman's eyes. The man shakes from cold. They are afraid to sit. They want immediate passage from this area so they can continue on toward freedom, but not tonight. First, they must rest, warm up, and eat. They need to be strong and healthy for the rest of their journey.

I warm the fire and prepare plates of food. I hand them bowls of stew. Gradually, they relax. We do not ask their names or where they are from. Perhaps they will tell their story later, perhaps not. Once a month or so, we receive visitors this way. Those who escape from southern states often travel weeks or months on their own, with little to guide them but the stars in the sky.

After dinner, they lie down and sleep soundly. My husband and I make plans. From our home in Baltimore, Maryland, the couple could travel as far west as the Ohio River Valley. That is where the

▲ *Runaway slaves sometimes traveled long distances until they were given shelter.*

Underground Railroad is most active. More fugitives than can be counted have cut a path from eastern Ohio through central Indiana.

They could also go north to Philadelphia or Boston. These two cities are major stops along the Underground Railroad. From there, we know people who can take the fugitives to Rochester or Buffalo, New York. Those cities are close to the United States' border. Just on the other side is Canada, the Promised Land.

We conductors move slowly and with caution. We travel from farm to farm, church to church, and home to home. Some conductors do no more than point the way. Others take fugitives many miles. From one hand to another, fugitives travel safely all the way to the Great Lakes and to Canada. We must be careful in Baltimore. Maryland is not a free state.

My husband and I follow the example of other conductors. Levi Coffin, who was born and raised in a slave state, now lives in Indiana. He formed a route from North Carolina to Indiana. We admire John Fairfield but don't dare behave like him. The man has no fear. Though born to a slave-owning family, Fairfield hates slavery. He has made many daring journeys to the South. He rescues family members of fugitives. He poses as a chicken peddler or a slave trader. In public, he pretends to be pro-slavery. Then he slips away with as many fugitives as he can.

George DeBaptiste is a black man who was born free in Virginia. In 1837, when he was 22 years old, he moved to Madison, Indiana, and opened a barbershop. There, near the Ohio River, he helps

HARRIET TUBMAN

Harriet Tubman became the most famous Underground Railroad conductor. She was born into slavery in Maryland in about the year 1820. (No records show her birth date.) In 1849, she ran away to Pennsylvania. She vowed to help others escape slavery. Risking her life, she returned to slave states at least 20 times. She led fugitives north, sometimes as far as Canada, and she never lost a single passenger.

fugitives escape from Kentucky. Many Underground Railroad conductors are freed slaves and fugitives. Some are even still slaves themselves.

In the morning, we learn the two fugitives came from the Carolinas. They escaped rather than be separated from each other and from their child when they were to be sold to other plantations. First, they fled to the Great Dismal Swamp. It is 1,000 square miles of peat bog and swamp. The place is so hard to wade through it is a perfect hiding place for fugitives. No one wants to go into it to catch runaway slaves.

They tried to find a so-called **maroon community** of escaped slaves. Instead, they got lost in the thick forests and muddy swamps. So, they headed north. They reached our home, and they are lucky they did not get caught. The new Fugitive Slave Act was pushed through Congress in September 1850. By law, citizens must force fugitives back to slavery. We ordinary citizens risk fines or jail time for helping fugitives. We risk fines for not harming them too, but no law can force me to be a slave catcher or stop what I'm doing.

We call these laws the Bloodhound Laws. Slave owners bring packs of dogs and hunt slaves like animals. The Fugitive Slave Act has made things far worse for runaways and for abolitionists. The country is going backward instead of forward, but we are not giving up. Like other conductors and station masters, I am willing to break laws I do not believe in.

SECOND SOURCE

▶ Find another source that describes the life of a conductor on the Underground Railroad. How does it compare and contrast to Emma Jackson's life?

My husband and I plan to take the fugitives north. We will go to the home of Gerrit Smith in Peterboro, New York. He is a prominent and outspoken abolitionist. He has made his home a station and is a reliable station master.

Since those new laws passed, many runaway slaves are fleeing to Canada. In Peterboro, New York, the couple and their child have a chance to reach Canada. As abolitionists, we know it will take more than politics and laws to end slavery, and we do not know how long it will take. We work to free as many people as we can, one by one.

ANALYZE THIS

▶ Find another narrative that details the dangers of taking part in the Underground Railroad. How is it similar to or different from what you read here?

LOOK, LOOK AGAIN

This image shows runaway slaves escaping north to freedom. Use this image to answer the following questions:

1. What would a fugitive slave think as he or she was traveling north? What would the hardest parts of the journey be?

2. How might a slave owner describe this scene?

3. How might an Underground Railroad conductor describe this scene to another abolitionist?

GLOSSARY

abolitionist (ab-uh-LISH-uh-nist) a person working to end slavery

compromise (KAHM-pruh-mize) to agree to something that is not entirely wanted, in order to address the requests of others

depot (DEE-poh) a railroad station

fugitive (FYOO-ji-tiv) a person who has escaped from something and is on the run

hierarchy (HYE-ur-ahr-kee) a system of rank, where some people are more important than others

maroon community (muh-ROON kuh-MYOO-ni-tee) a hidden community of escaped slaves

mode (MOHD) a method or way of doing something

plantation (plan-TAY-shuhn) a large farm where crops are grown on a large scale

principle (PRIN-suh-puhl) a basic truth or belief

LEARN MORE

Further Reading

Cross, L. D. *The Underground Railroad: The Long Journey to Freedom in Canada.* Toronto: J. Lorimer & Co., 2010.
Raatma, Lucia. *The Underground Railroad.* New York: Children's Press, 2011.
Sawyer, Kem Knapp. *Harriet Tubman.* New York: DK, 2010.

Web Sites

Aboard the Underground Railroad
http://www.nps.gov/nr/travel/underground/states.htm
This Web site includes a listing of key sites of the Underground Railroad by state.

The Underground Railroad: The Journey
http://education.nationalgeographic.com/education/multimedia/interactive/the-underground-railroad/?ar_a=1
This interactive Web site allows viewers to follow the Underground Railroad.

INDEX

ABOUT THE AUTHOR

Sheila Griffin Llanas is the author of many informational books for young readers. She lives in Wisconsin.